Who Was
Dr. Seuss?

This book belongs
to: Audrey♥
Pacheco

Who Was
Dr. Seuss?

By Janet B. Pascal
Illustrated by Nancy Harrison

Grosset & Dunlap
An Imprint of Penguin Group (USA) Inc.

For Diana, whom I often see
on the other Mulberry Street—JP

GROSSET & DUNLAP
Published by the Penguin Group
Penguin Group (USA) Inc., 375 Hudson Street, New York, New York 10014, USA
Penguin Group (Canada), 90 Eglinton Avenue East, Suite 700,
Toronto, Ontario M4P 2Y3, Canada (a division of Pearson Penguin Canada Inc.)
Penguin Books Ltd., 80 Strand, London WC2R 0RL, England
Penguin Group Ireland, 25 St. Stephen's Green, Dublin 2, Ireland
(a division of Penguin Books Ltd.)
Penguin Group (Australia), 250 Camberwell Road, Camberwell, Victoria 3124, Australia
(a division of Pearson Australia Group Pty. Ltd.)
Penguin Books India Pvt. Ltd., 11 Community Centre,
Panchsheel Park, New Delhi—110 017, India
Penguin Group (NZ), 67 Apollo Drive, Rosedale, Auckland 0632, New Zealand
(a division of Pearson New Zealand Ltd.)
Penguin Books (South Africa) (Pty.) Ltd., 24 Sturdee Avenue,
Rosebank, Johannesburg 2196, South Africa

Penguin Books Ltd., Registered Offices:
80 Strand, London WC2R 0RL, England

Text copyright © 2011 by Janet B. Pascal. Illustrations copyright © 2011 by Nancy Harrison. All rights reserved. Published by Grosset & Dunlap, a division of Penguin Young Readers Group, 345 Hudson Street, New York, New York 10014. GROSSET & DUNLAP is a trademark of Penguin Group (USA) Inc. Printed in the U.S.A.

Library of Congress Cataloging-in-Publication Data
Pascal, Janet B.
   Who was Dr. Seuss? / by Janet Pascal ; illustrated by Nancy Harrison.
      p. cm. — (Who was...?)
   Includes bibliographical references.
   ISBN 978-0-448-45585-3 (pbk.)
   1. Seuss, Dr.—Juvenile literature.   2. Authors, American—20th century—Biography—Juvenile literature.   3. Illustrators—United States—Biography—Juvenile literature.
   4. Children's literature—Authorship—Juvenile literature.
I. Harrison, Nancy, 1963- ill.   II. Title.
   PS3513.E2Z793   2011
   813'.52—dc22
   [B]   2010041738

ISBN 978-0-448-45585-3   10 9 8 7 6 5 4 3 2 1

Contents

Who Was
Dr. Seuss?

In 1985, Princeton University awarded honorary degrees to six people. An honorary degree is given to a person who has done something important for the world. The students were most excited about one of the people being honored. When a tall, thin

man with a gray beard stood up, they all leaped to their feet. "I am Sam," they chanted. "Sam-I-am." Then they recited, from memory, all of *Green Eggs and Ham*. It was a special way to show Theodor Geisel, better known as Dr. Seuss, how much his books meant to them.

Among the Princeton students that year was Michelle Robinson. Many years later, she married Barack Obama and became the First Lady of the United States. In 2010 she chose another Dr. Seuss book, *The Cat in the Hat*, to read aloud to the nation's schoolchildren. The First Lady knew that books for beginning readers used to be solemn and boring. Then Dr. Seuss appeared with his bouncy rhymes and wild and crazy characters like the Cat in the Hat, Horton, and the Grinch. Learning to read was never the same again.

Chapter 1
Goofy Machines

Theodor Seuss Geisel was born in Springfield, Massachusetts, on March 2, 1904. Springfield was full of factories turning out cars, guns, bicycles, tires, and toys. One of the factories was a brewery that Ted's grandfather had started called Kalmbach and Geisel. Ted's father became the president of the company. Its beer was so popular that the people of Springfield nicknamed the business "Come Back and Guzzle."

Ted grew up in a family that loved wordplay. His mother's family owned a bakery. As a child, she made up rhymes listing the pie flavors. Later, she sang her children to sleep with the same rhymes. Ted believed that his love of verse came from his memories of those pie poems.

His sister, two years older, was named
Margaretha. But she nicknamed herself "Marnie
Mecca Ding Ding Guy."

His father, also named Theodor, liked to
dream up goofy, complicated inventions in his
spare time. Ted's favorite was a "Silk-Stocking-
Back-Seam-Wrong-Detecting Mirror."

Young Ted loved to hang around the zoo. He got special treatment because his father helped run the zoo. Sometimes, he said, "they'd let me in the cage with the small lions and the small tigers, and I got chewed up every once in a while." (He was famous for exaggerating when he told stories.)

DO NOT FEED

After a visit to the zoo, Ted would rush home and draw animals on the walls of his room. Somehow the animals never ended up looking quite like what he had seen, so he would make up names for them. One of his mother's favorites was a creature with ears that were nine feet long. He called it a Wynnmph.

Like many people in Springfield, the Geisels came from Germany. Ted grew up speaking both German and English. In 1914, World War I started in Europe. Many countries were fighting against Germany. The United States was not in the war yet. (That didn't happen until 1917.) But Germans were becoming very unpopular in America.

At school, German American children were often bullied. Sometimes kids would throw rocks at Ted. The Geisel family tried hard to prove that

they were patriotic Americans. Ted's Boy Scout troop had a contest to see who could sell the most Liberty bonds—a way to help the government support the war effort. Ted's grandfather bought one thousand dollars worth. This made Ted one of the winners.

At the awards ceremony, medals were given out by former president Theodore Roosevelt. But someone in the Boy Scouts had made a mistake. There were ten winners, yet Roosevelt had only nine medals. When he ran out of medals, Ted was left standing alone onstage. Roosevelt bellowed, "What's this little boy doing here?" No one explained that Ted was a winner, too. Ted slunk away.

From then on, it was very hard for Ted to get up in front of people. Even after he was famous, he refused to give speeches. When he tried to appear on a television talk show, he was so scared that he couldn't say a word.

After the war ended in 1918, Ted's family faced a new problem. As 1920 began, Prohibition became the law in the United States. Prohibition meant that it was illegal to make or sell alcohol—including beer. The brewery had to close, and Ted's father was out of a job. The family still had enough to live on. But the loss of the brewery was a terrible blow. Now the family had much less

money, just as Ted was about to graduate from high school. But education was important to the Geisel family. No matter what, they made sure there was enough money for Ted to go to college.

Ted had never paid much attention to his schoolwork. He spent most of his time writing jokes for the school paper. The one class that interested him was English.

PROHIBITION

IN 1920 IT BECAME ILLEGAL TO SELL OR
MANUFACTURE ALCOHOL IN THE UNITED STATES.
THE EIGHTEENTH AMENDMENT, CALLED PROHIBITION,
WAS PASSED BY ACTIVISTS WHO THOUGHT
DRINKING LIQUOR WAS RUINING PEOPLE'S LIVES.
BUT PROHIBITION WAS NOT VERY SUCCESSFUL.
CRIME GROUPS SUCH AS THE MAFIA BECAME
MORE POWERFUL BY SMUGGLING LIQUOR.
GANGSTERS LIKE AL CAPONE BECAME FOLK
HEROES. MOST PEOPLE KEPT ON DRINKING, EVEN
THOUGH IT MEANT THEY WERE BREAKING THE LAW.
MANY TOWNS HAD A "SPEAKEASY," A PLACE
WHERE YOU COULD BUY ALCOHOLIC DRINKS IF YOU
KNEW THE SECRET PASSWORD OR KNOCK.

THE AMENDMENT WAS ESPECIALLY HARD ON PEOPLE LIKE THE GEISELS WHO HAD MADE THEIR LIVING SELLING ALCOHOL. (TED NEVER FORGOT WHAT IT DID TO HIS FAMILY. MANY OF HIS EARLY CARTOONS MADE FUN OF PROHIBITION.) CITIES THAT HAD BEEN FAMOUS FOR THEIR BREWERIES SUDDENLY LOST THEIR MOST IMPORTANT BUSINESSES—AND ALL THE TAX MONEY AND JOBS THAT WENT WITH THEM. SOME BREWERIES TRIED TO SURVIVE BY SELLING SODA. OTHER PLACES SOLD GRAPE JUICE OR MALT SYRUP. THEY INCLUDED CAREFUL INSTRUCTIONS TELLING THEIR CUSTOMERS EXACTLY WHAT *NOT* TO DO TO THEIR JUICE OR SYRUP TO MAKE SURE IT DIDN'T TURN INTO ALCOHOL. BY THE 1930S, IT WAS CLEAR THAT PROHIBITION WAS A FAILED EXPERIMENT. IN 1933, PRESIDENT FRANKLIN ROOSEVELT SIGNED A LAW THAT HELPED END IT. THEN HE SAID, "I THINK THIS WOULD BE A GOOD TIME FOR A BEER."

Ted's English teacher had gone to Dartmouth College in New Hampshire. He loved Dartmouth so much that Ted decided to go there, too.

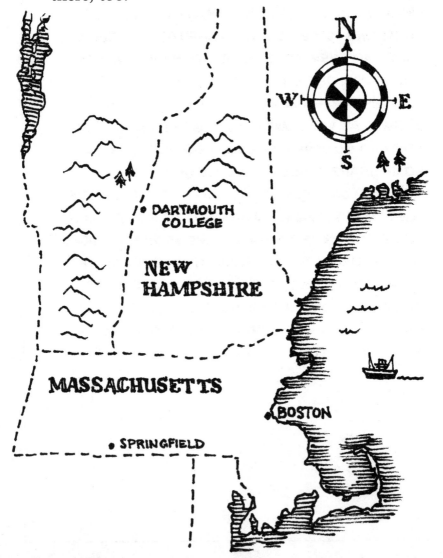

Chapter 2
A Very Fine Flying Cow

Ted loved Dartmouth. It was located in green countryside with beautiful old buildings. He made friends there who he kept for the rest of his life. Shortly after he arrived, he discovered the school humor magazine, *Jack-O-Lantern*, fondly known as *Jacko*. It became his dream to work

on *Jacko*, and he started spending all his time in the office. Staff members would find him there in the morning, fast asleep at his typewriter.

He was quickly elected to the staff and, at the end of his junior year, he was made editor in chief. The students loved his stories and drawings, and he became a very important person at Dartmouth. Even so, his classmates voted him

"Least Likely to Succeed." Ted never seemed to be serious about anything.

A month before graduation, Ted threw a party. The guests shared a bottle of gin. When a couple of boys began horsing around on the roof, Ted's landlord called the police. Because of Prohibition, gin was illegal, so Ted was in a lot of trouble.

As punishment, he was not allowed to write for *Jacko* anymore. But he found a way around this. He signed his work with fake names. He had already used joke names such as Oo-La-La McCarty and Theo LeSieg (LeSieg was Geisel spelled backward). Now he started using just his middle name, Seuss.

At Dartmouth, Ted had spent all his time on *Jacko*. His grades were not very good. Ted's father was afraid that he wouldn't be able to get a job after college. But Ted told his dad not to worry. He was going to Oxford, a famous university in England. What's more, he said, he had won a prize to pay for it! His father was so thrilled that he told the local newspaper. The next day, Ted was headline news.

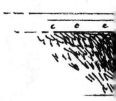

But there was a problem. Ted *had* applied to Oxford. But he hadn't really won any money. He only hoped he would. Ted had to tell his father the truth. The older Geisel was a very proud man. He had already announced to the world that Ted was going to Oxford. So he decided that he would have to pay for his son to go. In the summer of 1925, Ted boarded a steamship for the long journey to England.

Ted never really fit in at Oxford. The university was about eight hundred years old. All the students seemed very serious. The lectures bored him. Ted tried to listen and take notes, but his mind wandered. Instead, he doodled. The pages of his notebooks were filled with chickens with windmill tails, dogs walking across tightropes, and cows with wings.

Helen Palmer, another American, was at Oxford studying to be a teacher. One day she looked over Ted's shoulder to see what he was drawing.

"That's a very fine flying cow!" she said.

Helen told Ted his drawings were special. She said he should be an illustrator. Helen's remark changed Ted's life. He realized he didn't want to teach. He didn't want to write novels. He just wanted to keep drawing his mixed-up animals. After that, Ted and Helen spent all their time together. One day, he proposed and Helen accepted. But they couldn't get married yet. They didn't have any money.

After she graduated from Oxford, Helen took a teaching job in New Jersey. Ted dropped out of school and moved back in with his parents in Springfield, MA. He knew what he wanted to do with his life. Now he just had to figure out how to make a living from his drawings.

Chapter 3
Boids and Beasties

Back at his parents' house, Ted spent his time drawing cartoons and writing funny articles. He sent them to everyone he could think of—magazines in New York, college friends, advertising agencies. But no one except Helen seemed to be interested in flying cows and dancing dogs.

Then a famous magazine, the *Saturday Evening Post,* accepted a cartoon. Ted had drawn two elegant tourists with parasols. They were sitting on tame camels and imagining that they were brave explorers. He signed it, simply, "Seuss."

The *Post* paid him twenty-five dollars. Even in 1927, that wasn't a lot of money. But it would pay for a month's rent. Ted decided it was

enough to show he could earn a living as an
illustrator. He moved to New York City. But
until he had a steady income, he still couldn't
marry Helen. Instead Ted shared an apartment
with a friend from Dartmouth. It was cheap

and dirty. Every night before they went
to bed, they had to take canes and
whack away the rats.

Ted's roommate knew someone who worked for a humor magazine called *Judge*. He introduced Ted, and the magazine offered him a job. He would be a writer and artist and earn a salary.

Now he and Helen could marry. They had to change the date of their wedding once because Ted's sister, Marnie, was about to give birth. Ted wanted his whole family to be able to come to his wedding. Ted's niece, Peggy, was born on November 1, 1927. On November 29, Ted and Helen were married in her parents' parlor.

Ted became very popular at *Judge*. He started writing a column called "Boids and Beasties," where he could introduce all his strange, playful creatures. He signed the column, "Dr. Seuss." He added the "Dr." because he had disappointed his father by dropping out of Oxford.

Unfortunately, *Judge* magazine was having money troubles. They didn't always have enough cash to pay their staff. Companies paid for ads in *Judge* with samples of their products instead of money. These samples got passed on to the staff as their salaries. Often Ted was paid in cases of shaving cream or soda. Once he received 1,872 nail clippers. That wasn't much help in paying the costs of everyday life.

Then, in 1928, he had a stroke of luck. It started with Flit, a popular bug killer. Before air-conditioning, people had to leave their windows open in the summer to let in cool breezes. Houses became full of bugs. Ted started thinking about how awful summer must have been for the knights of old. It was bad enough having bugs inside—what if dragons could fly in and bite you?

He drew a cartoon showing a knight in armor who can't get to sleep because there is a dragon in his room. The caption says: "Darn it all, another dragon. And just after I'd sprayed the whole castle with Flit."

The wife of an advertising executive for Flit was at a beauty salon where she happened to see the cartoon in a magazine. She loved it so much, she made her husband hire Ted to do all the Flit ads.

Ted drew people in funny situations being attacked by huge bugs. This became one of the most successful advertising campaigns in history.

Today, few people remember the tagline Ted invented: "Quick, Henry, the Flit!" But from the late twenties to the fifties, *everyone* knew it. Comedians quoted it, and it appeared in popular songs. Sales of Flit shot way up. And Dr. Seuss's drawings became famous.

Flit hired Ted at a salary of twelve thousand dollars a year—a lot of money at the time. The next year, the stock market crashed, and America plunged into the Great Depression. All over the country, people were out of work, poor, and starving. But thanks to Flit, Ted had plenty of money.

With his new wealth, he and Helen began throwing parties. They had a very active social life, and Ted became famous in their circle of friends for his practical jokes. Once he sneaked

into the kitchen and put a huge plastic pearl in one of the oysters that was going to be served at dinner. Another time, he filled a friend's bathtub with Jell-O and goldfish.

In 1931, Ted's mother died at the age of fifty-two. Her early death was a shock to Ted. But at least she had lived long enough to see his first big success.

Flit made Ted financially secure for life, but there was one problem: He didn't want to spend all his time drawing Flit ads. But his contract wouldn't let him do most other kinds of work. Years later he wrote, "I would like to say I went into children's book work because of my great understanding of children." But it wasn't really true. Actually, illustrating children's books was one of the few things his contract let him do.

NEW YORK APARTMENTS

THE GEISELS' FIRST APARTMENT IN MANHATTAN WAS RIGHT ACROSS THE STREET FROM A HORSE STABLE. SOON THEY MOVED TO A BETTER APARTMENT. THEIR NEW PHONE NUMBER WAS ONLY ONE DIGIT DIFFERENT FROM A NEARBY FISH STORE. THEY OFTEN GOT TELEPHONE CALLS FROM PEOPLE WHO WANTED TO BUY FISH. INSTEAD OF TELLING THEM THEY HAD THE WRONG NUMBER, TED WOULD DRAW A PICTURE OF THE FISH THEY HAD ORDERED AND DELIVER IT. NOT EVERYONE WAS AMUSED AT THE TIME, BUT JUST THINK WHAT THOSE DRAWINGS WOULD BE WORTH TODAY!

Chapter 4
What I Saw on Mulberry Street

An editor at Viking Books saw the Flit
advertisements and hired Ted to illustrate a book
of mistakes made by schoolchildren. So Ted found
himself drawing pictures for silly quotations
like, "Benjamin Franklin produced electricity by
rubbing cats backward." The book was published
in 1931. To Ted's surprise, it became a big hit—
and Viking signed him
up to do a sequel.

Ted soon realized he'd make more money if he wrote and illustrated his own books. He began looking for the perfect subject for his first book.

In 1936, Ted and Helen took a trip to Europe. On the ship ride home, he scribbled picture book ideas in his notebook—ideas like "a stupid horse and wagon" and "flying cat pulling Viking ship." Nothing seemed quite right. Meanwhile, the throbbing noise of the ship's engines was driving him crazy. He started fitting words to it. Suddenly he found himself chanting, "And *that* is a *sto*ry that *no* one can *beat*. And to *think* that I *saw* it on *Mul*berry *Street*."

And there was his story. A little boy walking home on Mulberry Street—a main street in Ted's hometown—looks for something interesting to tell his father about. All he can see is "a plain horse and wagon." But by the time he reaches his house, he has turned the horse and wagon into a whole circus parade, with blue elephants and a brass band.

All the rhymes in Dr. Seuss's books bounce along so naturally that people think they must have been easy to write. But Ted worked hard. "I know my stuff looks like it was all rattled off in twenty-eight seconds," he complained, "but every word is a struggle." For one picture book, he might write and tear up five hundred or even one thousand pages.

Finally Ted was happy with *And to Think That I Saw It on Mulberry Street*. He started sending it to publishers. They all rejected it. Most editors found it just too different. They thought the verse was rough and silly. Worst of all, it didn't have a moral. It wouldn't help make children behave better. "What's wrong with kids having fun reading without being preached at?" Ted yelled.

Ted was about to give up when he ran into another Dartmouth friend. Marshall McClintock had just that day become the children's book editor for Vanguard Press. Vanguard often published books that were "different." They were delighted with the book and immediately said yes. Ted was so grateful, he named the hero in the book "Marco" after McClintock's son.

Chapter 5
An Elephant up a Tree

Reviewers loved *Mulberry Street*, and it sold very well—for a children's book. But during the Depression, people didn't have a lot of money to spend on children's books. To make a living, Ted had to keep doing ads. He said he couldn't tell if he was a real author or "just a lowly advertising man."

His second book was inspired by one of his favorite things—hats. He and Helen liked to travel. Everywhere they went, he would buy hats—maybe a fireman's hat from Peru or a fancy European helmet. Sometimes when he got stuck while writing, he would put on a hat as a "thinking cap." One day Ted would invent the most famous hat of all and put it on a cat, but for now, he

wrote *The 500 Hats of Bartholomew Cubbins.*

Ted and Helen had
recently learned they could
not have children. Later,
Ted said he hadn't wanted
kids, anyway. They made
him nervous. "You have 'em,
I'll amuse 'em," he would tell

people. But his niece believed that, really, he would have loved to have had a child.

He dealt with the sad news in his own way. He invented a daughter named Chrysanthemum-Pearl and dedicated his new book to her. He and Helen sometimes included Chrysanthemum-Pearl on their Christmas cards, along with other imaginary children such as Norval, Wickersham, and Thnud.

To
Chrysanthemum-Pearl
(aged 89 months, going on 90)

With two children's books out, the name of Dr. Seuss was becoming well-known. Ted had always pronounced his name in the German fashion: "Zoyce." But most of his readers said "Soose." Ted liked that this rhymed with Mother Goose, so he started saying "Soose," too.

Random House, a much bigger publisher than
Vanguard, became interested in Dr. Seuss. The
head of Random House, Bennett Cerf, promised
to publish anything Ted wrote. How could he
resist? He was sad to leave his friends at Vanguard.
But he loved Random House. They stayed his
publisher for the rest of his life. Over the years, he
became close friends with many of the people
he worked with there.

His first book for them was not what Random House hoped for. *The Seven Lady Godivas* was for grown-ups and was full of pictures of naked ladies. This was not Ted's strong point, and Bennett Cerf didn't think the book was very good. Still he kept his promise to let Ted publish whatever he wanted. The book was a complete flop. Ted went back to children's books.

One day around 1939 (at least as he told the
story), Ted left his window open. The wind blew
around some doodles he had left out. When he

came back, there was a drawing of an elephant on top of a drawing of a tree. Why would an elephant be in a tree? Was he hatching an egg? Ted named the elephant Horton, but he got stuck trying to figure out what should happen to him.

"I'm very upset," Helen told a friend, "because Ted has that elephant up a tree, and he doesn't know how he's going to get him down." It was Helen who finally came up with an ending. Horton would hatch an elephant-bird—like the flying cow she had once seen doodled in Ted's notebook.

Ted loved *Horton Hatches the Egg* more than anything else he'd written. He told his editor that it was the funniest children's book ever. Everyone else loved it, too. Horton the elephant is still one of Dr. Seuss's most beloved characters.

But by the time the book came out in 1940, Ted was not thinking about elephant-birds. He was worried and unhappy about what was going on in the world around him. World War II had broken out in Europe. His parents' homeland, Germany, was now controlled by Adolf Hitler and the Nazis. Hitler wanted to rule all of Europe. Most Americans still hoped the United States could stay out of the war, but not Ted. Even though he hated war, the Nazis had to be stopped. If his funny drawings could convince people to buy Flit, could they convince them to fight Hitler? Ted turned his attention to the war and did not write another children's book for seven years.

Chapter 6
Private SNAFU

Ted began drawing political cartoons that criticized people who thought America should stay out of the war. He showed them as ostriches burying their heads in the sand, ignoring the danger around them.

On December 7, 1941, Germany's ally, Japan, bombed Pearl Harbor in Hawaii, and the United States entered the war. Now Ted felt that just drawing cartoons wasn't enough. At thirty-eight,

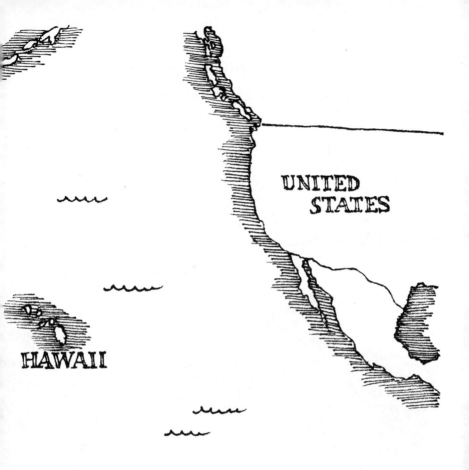

UNITED
STATES

HAWAII

he was old to be a soldier, but he enlisted in the
army, anyway. The army knew exactly what to do
with a gentle, clumsy artist who couldn't shoot a
gun. He was sent to Hollywood, California. There

he made movies to train new soldiers.

Ted didn't know anything about making movies, but he knew how to hold people's interest. He helped create the Private SNAFU cartoons. Private SNAFU was a lazy, careless soldier who did everything wrong. (SNAFU stands for "Situation Normal, All Fouled Up.") Private SNAFU showed soldiers what *not* to do.

Later, Ted was promoted to working on live films. He helped write two films about what the US should do in Germany and Japan after the war was won. Revised versions of the films both won Oscars. But today they are completely unknown.

With two Oscars to his credit, Ted thought maybe he would work on movies instead of books. But he quickly changed his mind. He saw that the postwar world would be full of promise as well as danger. He decided nothing was more important than writing children's books. "The new generations *must* grow up to be more intelligent than *ours*," he wrote.

THE QUESTION OF WAR

AT THE BEGINNING OF 1941, EIGHTY PERCENT OF AMERICANS WERE AGAINST THE IDEA OF THE UNITED STATES JOINING THE WAR AGAINST GERMANY. WITH AN ENTIRE OCEAN SEPARATING AMERICA FROM EUROPE, THESE PEOPLE—CALLED ISOLATIONISTS—FELT THAT THE TROUBLES IN EUROPE WERE VERY FAR AWAY. THEY BELIEVED THAT THE DUTY OF THE UNITED STATES WAS TO PROTECT ITSELF.

BUT TED DID NOT FEEL ISOLATED FROM THE FIGHTING IN EUROPE. HE SAID, "WHILE PARIS WAS BEING OCCUPIED BY THE CLANKING TANKS OF THE NAZIS . . . I FOUND I COULD NO LONGER KEEP MY MIND ON DRAWING PICTURES OF HORTON THE ELEPHANT." IN HIS POLITICAL CARTOONS, TED TRIED TO SHOW HOW CLOSELY THE COUNTRIES OF THE WORLD WERE CONNECTED TO ONE ANOTHER. IN ONE DRAWING, HE SHOWED UNCLE SAM HAPPILY TAKING A BATH. UNCLE SAM IS THINKING, "THE OLD FAMILY BATHTUB IS PLENTY SAFE FOR ME." BECAUSE HIS EYES ARE SHUT, HE DOES NOT SEE THAT THE TUB IS FILLED WITH A SHARK, A CROCODILE, AND A POISONOUS BUG READY TO CHOMP ON HIM.

Chapter 7
A Moose, a Nerd, and the Whos

MARNIE

Ted's joy at the end of World War II was cut short by the death of his sister, Marnie. Because of a family quarrel, she and Ted had fallen out of touch. She died before they could make up. Her death upset him so much that he avoided talking about her for the rest of his life.

Now that the war was over, Ted and Helen decided to stay in California. They bought an old observation tower on a mountain outside La Jolla, a beautiful California town on the Pacific coast. For years, the tower had been empty, and it was a favorite meeting place for young couples. The walls were covered with carved initials. Even after the Geisels moved in, some couples would still try to come inside.

One of Ted's first books after the war was *Thidwick the Big-Hearted Moose*. Thidwick is too nice and lets other animals push him around. At

the end of the story, Ted asks readers, "Well, what would YOU do if it happened to YOU?" Ted ended many of his books this way, by asking questions. He wanted kids to enjoy his stories. But he also wanted to help them think for themselves.

Ted began to turn out one or two books every year. They were funny, original, and very different from one another. People often asked Ted where he got his ideas. He said that he usually started by doodling. "I may doodle a couple of animals. If they bite each other, it's going to be a good book." After a while he got tired of this question. He started saying that he got his ideas from the people in a small town "called Über Gletch. I go there on the fourth of August every summer to get my cuckoo clock repaired." From then on, he gave this answer to everyone—even President John F. Kennedy's wife, Jacqueline.

Some of his books were inspired by the real world. In 1953, *Life* magazine sent Ted and Helen to Japan to find out how the country was coping after the war. Ted had mixed feelings about the Japanese. In his wartime cartoons, he had shown Japanese people—even US citizens—as villains.

But as he talked to teachers and schoolchildren in Japan, he got past this prejudice. He saw that the people of Japan were trying to honor the importance of each individual and still work together for the common good.

Back in his studio, Ted explored what he had learned in Japan. To do this, he returned to one of his most beloved characters—Horton the elephant. In *Horton Hears a Who!*, Horton must save the tiny world of Who-ville by proving it exists. He can do this only by getting every Who, even the very smallest and laziest, to work together. Horton is willing to risk everything for the Whos because "a person's a person no matter how small." Ted dedicated the book to a Japanese friend.

By the time *Horton Hears a Who!* was published, personal troubles had taken over Ted's life. Helen was suffering from a terrible illness. She could not breathe on her own and had to be put in an iron lung—a huge metal case that enclosed most of her body. Ted spent hours sitting beside her in the hospital. When she came home, Ted rigged up mirrors so Helen could watch their dog playing outside.

Ted had relied on Helen for everything. She helped him with all his books and ran his life for him. Without her, he didn't even know how to balance a checkbook.

Helen amazed her doctors by recovering almost completely. By May 1955, she was able to travel back to Dartmouth with Ted to see him get an honorary doctorate. Years ago, he had disappointed his father by not earning a degree from Oxford. But now he made up for it. He was no longer just Dr. Seuss, he boasted. He was *Dr.* Dr. Seuss.

THE FIRST NERD

TED LOVED TO INVENT WORDS LIKE *THNEED* AND *SALA-MA-GOO*. ONE OF HIS WORDS ESCAPED FROM ITS BOOK AND BECAME PART OF THE ENGLISH LANGUAGE. DR. SEUSS WAS THE FIRST PERSON TO USE THE WORD *NERD*. IN *IF I RAN THE ZOO*, PUBLISHED IN 1959, YOUNG GERALD MCGREW PLANS TO "SAIL TO KA-TROO AND BRING BACK . . . A NERD." NO ONE KNOWS QUITE HOW IT HAPPENED, BUT WITHIN A YEAR, TEENAGERS IN DETROIT WERE USING *NERD* TO MEAN "A DRIP OR SQUARE," AND SOON THE NEW WORD HAD SPREAD ACROSS THE WHOLE COUNTRY.

Chapter 8
The Cat in the Hat Arrives

In 1954, an article appeared in *Life*, a popular weekly magazine. It asked why American children had so much trouble learning to read.

Was it because books for beginning readers were so boring? Teachers thought children learned to read by seeing the same words over and over. So early readers used short, choppy sentences that just kept repeating the same thing. Why would smart children read these dull books? If someone like Dr. Seuss wrote an early reader, maybe children would actually want to read it.

A friend of Ted's, William Spaulding, worked for the publisher Houghton Mifflin. He read the article and said to Ted, "Write me a story that first-graders can't put down!" Ted was willing to try. Random House and Houghton Mifflin worked out an agreement. Houghton Mifflin would sell the book to schools and libraries, and Random House would sell it to bookstores.

William Spaulding gave Ted a list of about three hundred words that most first-graders should know. The book could only use about 225

words, and all of them had to come from this list. Ted thought it would be easy to toss off a little story—but he soon found out it was almost impossible. Every time he had an idea, he needed a word that wasn't on the list. He spent more than a year trying and failing. Finally he decided, "I'll read [the list] once more and if I can find two words that rhyme, that will be my book." He found them—*cat* and *hat*—and *The Cat in the Hat* was born.

The Cat in the Hat was published in 1957. Many teachers didn't like it. They thought it looked too much like a comic book and it wasn't serious. Some librarians hid it and hoped kids wouldn't find it. Houghton Mifflin, which handled school and library sales, didn't sell many copies.

But kids loved *The Cat in the Hat*. They read it and told their friends about it. Bookstores

couldn't keep it on the shelves. It just kept selling and never stopped. Within three years, it had sold over one million copies. Of everything he had ever written, Ted said, "It's the book I'm proudest of . . ."

At Random House, Bennett Cerf's wife, Phyllis, thought *The Cat in the Hat* should be just the beginning. She wanted to publish a whole series of books like it—books that used just a few words but were so much fun kids would actually want to read them. She convinced her husband to let her start a new company at Random House. It would be run by Phyllis, Ted, and Helen. Called Beginner Books, it would publish beginning readers by Dr. Seuss and also by other people.

Right away, Beginner Books was a hit. Random House became the nation's largest publisher of children's books. Ted was happy to publish books by old friends from his army days, like P. D. Eastman, who wrote *Are You My*

Mother? and *Go, Dog. Go!* He also published a
book by Marshall McClintock, the Vanguard
editor who had given him his start years before.
And he discovered books about a family of bears
written by Stan and Jan Berenstain.

Bennett Cerf was amused by the word list
Beginner Books authors had to use. If writing a
book using only three hundred words was so
hard, he asked, what about one with even fewer?

He bet Ted fifty dollars that he couldn't write a book using only fifty words. Bennett Cerf lost his bet. Ted wrote and illustrated *Green Eggs and Ham* using exactly fifty words. It remains the most popular of all his books and the fourth best-selling children's book of all time.

THE BABY BOOM

BEGINNER BOOKS BEGAN AT THE BEST POSSIBLE TIME. AFTER WORLD WAR II, AMERICAN FAMILIES STARTED HAVING LOTS OF CHILDREN. BY 1957, THERE WERE MORE KIDS JUST LEARNING TO READ THAN EVER BEFORE. AT THE SAME TIME, THE UNITED STATES WAS MORE AND MORE AFRAID OF THE USSR, A GROUP OF COMMUNIST COUNTRIES. PEOPLE WERE WORRIED THAT SCHOOLS IN THESE COUNTRIES WERE BETTER AT TRAINING CHILDREN TO BECOME SCIENTISTS AND INVENTORS. SO IN 1958, THE US GOVERNMENT BEGAN TO POUR MONEY INTO SCHOOLS AND LIBRARIES. SOME OF THIS MONEY WAS USED TO BUY BOOKS LIKE DR. SEUSS'S BEGINNER BOOKS SERIES.

Chapter 9
Grinches and Turtles and Sneetches

In 1957 *The Cat in the Hat* turned Ted into a superstar author. He had become the head of his own publishing house. As if that wasn't enough for one year, he also invented the Grinch.

Ted liked to hint that the Grinch was Dr. Seuss himself. He even had a license plate that said "GRINCH." As for where the name came from, he said, "I just drew him and looked at him, and it was obvious to me who he was."

As soon as it was published, *How the Grinch Stole Christmas!* was a big hit. A few years later, Ted got a call from an old friend, Chuck Jones. He was now a famous animator, and the creator of Road Runner and Wile E. Coyote. He wanted to make a version of the Grinch for TV. Ted was

uneasy about the idea, but he trusted Jones. He even let him turn the Grinch green. (He had been black-and-white with pink eyes in the book.) The Grinch Christmas special appeared on TV in 1966 and has been a holiday favorite ever since.

Ted and Helen finally had exactly the life they wanted. They had plenty of money, so Ted didn't have to do any more ads. Helen was happy to take care of all the practical details of life so he could just write and draw **PEGGY** all day. They did not have family of their own, but they became close with Ted's niece, Peggy.

Ted had loved playing with Peggy when she was a baby. Even after he and Marnie were not speaking, he kept in touch with Peggy. In her

twenties, Peggy moved out to California. She lived in the Geisel's tower for a while. She even got married there. Her son, another Ted, named Teddy, was like a grandson to the Geisels. He was quiet and gentle like Ted, and he wanted to be an artist. Teddy was one of the few people Ted would allow into the studio while he was working.

Over the next ten years, Ted wrote twelve books, including classics like *The Cat in the Hat*

Comes Back, One Fish Two Fish Red Fish Blue Fish, and *Hop on Pop!*

All of Ted's stories were a lot of fun, but they also brought up serious ideas. *Yertle the Turtle and Other Stories* is about a tyrant who pushes everyone around and an ordinary little turtle who is brave enough to stand up to him. Ted based *Yertle* on Hitler, and he worried that people might object to this. But actually, the only problem came when the little turtle burps. "Nobody had ever burped before on the pages of a children's book," Ted explained.

Another book that meant a lot to him was *The Sneetches and Other Stories*. During the early 1960s, black people were struggling to win their civil rights. In his book, Ted described all the trouble between the star-bellied Sneetches and the Sneetches without stars. The story shows how silly Ted thought it was for people to hate one another because they looked different.

It was hard work writing all those books. Ted spent eight hours a day at his desk, seven days a week. He said that he did his best work when he wrote himself into a corner—"so there was seemingly no way of ending the book"—and then had to write his way out.

Helen had to deal with Ted's moods while he was doing this. She explained, "About two weeks before the completion of every book he . . . decides that nothing in the book is any good . . ." Then she had to talk him out of throwing the whole thing away.

After he finished a book, he was just as bad. He would worry, "I'm never going to write anything, I've lost it, I just can't do it." Then one of his doodles would start his mind moving, and he'd be happy again.

Work was always the center of Ted's life. But sometimes he did take a break. He and Helen enjoyed traveling all over the world. They looked at elephant seals in Mexico. In Peru, they helped search for mummies. They went to Australia, Africa, and Hawaii.

HOW DO YOU SAY *GRINCH* IN CHINESE?

圣诞怪杰

AT FIRST, DR. SEUSS'S BOOKS WERE NOT WELL-KNOWN OUTSIDE THE UNITED STATES. PEOPLE IN ENGLAND THOUGHT THEY WERE TOO "AMERICAN"—VULGAR, RUDE, AND SLANGY. AND IT WAS HARD TO INTRODUCE THE BOOKS TO OTHER COUNTRIES BECAUSE DR. SEUSS'S RHYMES AND INVENTED WORDS WERE ALMOST IMPOSSIBLE TO TRANSLATE. CLEVER TRANSLATORS TRIED, HOWEVER, AND SOON DR. SEUSS'S FAME SPREAD AROUND THE WHOLE WORLD. EVENTUALLY HIS BOOKS APPEARED IN MORE THAN TWENTY LANGUAGES, INCLUDING CHINESE, SWEDISH, SPANISH, HEBREW, MAORI, LATIN, JAPANESE, GREEK, AND YIDDISH.

At home, they loved to entertain. Guests would gather around the piano and sing. Sometimes the Geisels set up special treats, like a helicopter ride around the California coast. And Ted and his friends still loved to play practical jokes on one another.

The business of being famous took up more and more of Ted's time. In 1957 alone, he received almost a thousand pounds of fan mail. Helen answered most of it. She signed her letters "Mrs. Dr. Seuss."

Ted was still terrified of speaking in public, but now that he was so famous, sometimes he had to. He found that he could do it as long as the speech was in verse. He once explained to a big group of booksellers: "As everyone present undoubtedly knows . . . I am completely incapable of speaking in prose."

Chapter 10
I Speak for the Trees

After many happy years together, Helen began struggling with illness and depression again. On October 23, 1967, she died. She was sixty-eight years old. For forty years, she had taken care of everything for Ted. She handled money matters, shielded him from publicity, and went over every line he wrote. He did not know how to live life alone. He needed a companion. In 1968, he married Audrey Dimond, a close friend of the Geisels for many years.

Ted enjoyed pointing out that when he first met Audrey, not only had she never read any of his books, she had never heard of Dr. Seuss. When he was introduced—as "our very own dear Dr. Seuss"—she assumed he was a medical doctor.

Audrey quickly became interested in his work, however, and soon she was discussing every detail with him, just as Helen had done. Shortly after Ted and Audrey were married, Ted's father died at the age of eighty-nine. For years Ted had worried that he was a disappointment to his father. Sometimes they did not speak to each other for a long time. But as Ted became more successful and happy with his

life, they had
become good
friends. Ted
always treasured
the enormous stone

dinosaur footprint his father had given him. He
carried it with him from house to house all his life.

By 1970, the view of La Jolla from Ted's tower
window had changed. Once he had looked out
on beaches and trees, but now the land was
covered with houses

and apartments. He decided he had to write a book about caring for the natural world. For the first time, the message for his book came to him before the story or characters.

Writing *The Lorax*, Ted said, was "the hardest thing I have ever done." He had read so many facts, and he cared so much about the natural world, that the story kept turning into a lecture. When he was completely stuck, Audrey said to him, "Let's go to Africa."

In Kenya, Ted was excited to discover trees that looked just like the puffy ones he had invented for his new book. "They've stolen my truffula trees!" he exclaimed. On a safari trip, he saw a herd of wild elephants ambling by. Suddenly

he knew exactly what he wanted to say. He grabbed some scrap paper and wrote almost the whole story in one sitting.

The Lorax tells the story of a beautiful land where truffula trees grow. The Once-ler wants to chop them all down to use in his factories. It is the Lorax who "speaks for the trees." It was Ted's favorite of all his books, but it didn't sell very well at first. People thought it preached too much. A few years later, when saving the environment was on everyone's mind, the book found its audience.

In 1989, *The Lorax* became the first Dr. Seuss book to encounter censorship. The logging industry wanted it off school reading lists. But Ted argued that he wasn't against logging or industry. "I live in a house made of wood and write books printed on paper," he pointed out.

He was just against the greed that made people go too far and ignore the damage they caused.

In 1984, *The Butter Battle Book* came out. It, too, made some people angry. It tells the story of the Yooks and the Zooks, enemies who keep building bigger and more complicated weapons to fight against each other. Finally they each have a weapon that could destroy everyone. They stand facing each other, wondering what will happen next. Ted didn't feel he could write a comforting happy ending. After all, in the real world, the United States and the USSR were both trying to build bigger, better weapons. So in *The Butter Battle Book*, Ted left it up to his readers to think about how the story should end.

Some people wanted this book taken off of library shelves. Ted had worked hard to convince the United States to fight in World War II. How could he write a book against war? Audrey comforted him by telling him, "You're not just writing books for children, you're writing for humanity." The book's success proved her point. It was the first children's book ever to spend six months on the adult best seller list of the *New York Times Book Review.*

Ted liked to joke that he was responsible for the end of the Cold War. In 1990, a version of *The Butter Battle Book* was televised in the Soviet Union. "Right after that," Ted pointed out, "the USSR began falling apart."

Chapter 11
Oh, the Places You'll Go!

The same year he wrote *The Butter Battle Book*, Ted received a great honor—a Pulitzer Prize. This prize for American writing had never been given to a children's book writer. He was so surprised that he had a hard time convincing himself it wasn't a hoax.

In 1990, he published *Oh, the Places You'll Go!*, summing up his view of life. The illustrations sum up his work, too. If you look carefully, there are details from his earlier books everywhere. Dr. Seuss speaks to his readers directly throughout the whole story, describing all the challenges and adventures facing a young person starting out on the road of life. He ends cheerfully, but he doesn't make any promises: "And will you succeed? Yes, you will indeed! (98 and ¾ percent guaranteed.)"

Ted realized this book would probably be his last. He was almost eighty-six years old. For most of his life, he had been a heavy smoker. He was never able to break the habit, even after his dentist found cancer in his mouth. Less than two years later, on September 24, 1991, Ted Geisel died at the age of eighty-seven. One of the last things he told his wife was, "I've had a wonderful life. I've done what I had to do. I lived where I wished to live. I had love. I had everything."

As Ted had wanted, he had no funeral and no grave. But people everywhere mourned him and remembered him with love. At Dartmouth, the students and teachers sat outside for twenty-four hours reading his books aloud.

Even after Ted Geisel's death, Dr. Seuss lived on. During the course of his career, he wrote some forty books. In 2001, when *Publishers Weekly* drew

up a list of the top 150 best-selling children's books of all time, twenty-four were by Dr. Seuss.

Ted's longtime agent estimated that something by Dr. Seuss is the first book given to one out of every four children born in the United States. And *Oh, the Places You'll Go!* is one of the most popular gifts for high school and college graduates. So today, over a century after Theodor Geisel was born, most American childhoods begin and end with Dr. Seuss.

TIMELINE OF
THEODOR SEUSS GEISEL'S LIFE

1904 — Theodor Seuss Geisel born on March 2

1921–1925 — Attends Dartmouth College

1927 — Marries Helen Palmer

1928 — Begins drawing "Quick, Henry, the Flit!" advertisements

1931 — Dr. Seuss illustrations appear in a book for the first time

1937 — Publishes his first book, *And to Think That I Saw It on Mulberry Street*

1943 — Joins the United States Army Motion Picture Unit

1954 — Publishes *Horton Hears a Who!*

1957 — Publishes *The Cat in the Hat* and *How the Grinch Stole Christmas!* and becomes president of Beginner Books

1960 — Publishes *Green Eggs and Ham*

1966 — *How the Grinch Stole Christmas!* appears on TV

1968 — Marries Audrey Dimond

1984 — Wins special Pulitzer Prize for contribution to children's literature

1991 — Dr. Seuss dies on September 24

TIMELINE OF THE WORLD

The United States begins work on the Panama Canal — **1904**

World War I begins — **1914**

World War I ends — **1918**

Prohibition begins in the United States — **1920**

Beginning of the Great Depression — **1929**

Prohibition repealed — **1933**

First appearance of Daffy Duck, in a Looney Tunes film — **1937**

World War II begins — **1939**

World War II ends — **1945**

Brown v. Board of Education makes racial segregation — **1954**
of schools illegal in the United States

Soviet Union launches *Sputnik 1* and *2*; — **1957**
Wham-O makes the first Frisbee

United States Civil Rights Act is passed — **1964**

United States' *Apollo 11* is the first manned mission — **1969**
to land on the moon

Microsoft is founded — **1975**

Soviet Union collapses — **1991**